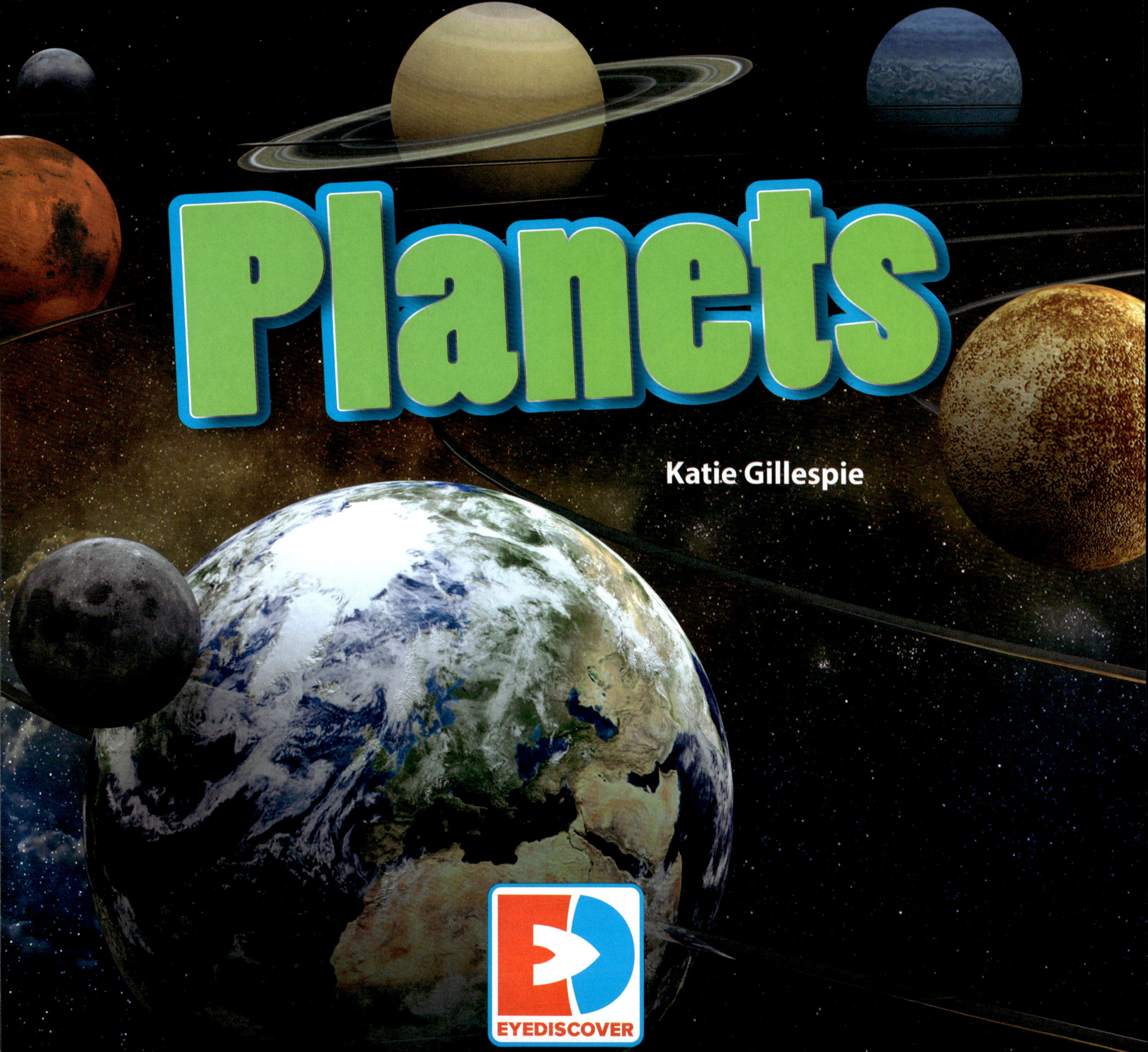
Planets
Katie Gillespie
EYEDISCOVER

Go to www.eyediscover.com and enter this book's unique code.

BOOK CODE

X274953

EYEDISCOVER brings you optic readalongs that support active learning.

Published by AV² by Weigl
350 5th Avenue, 59th Floor New York, NY 10118
Website: www.eyediscover.com

Library of Congress Control Number: 2017930721

ISBN 978-1-4896-5677-3 (hardcover)

Printed in the United States of America
in Brainerd, Minnesota
1 2 3 4 5 6 7 8 9 0 21 20 19 18 17

072017
020317

Editor: Katie Gillespie
Designer: Mandy Christiansen

Weigl acknowledges Getty Images and iStock as the primary image suppliers for this title.

EYEDISCOVER provides enriched content, optimized for tablet use, that supplements and complements this book. EYEDISCOVER books strive to create inspired learning and engage young minds in a total learning experience.

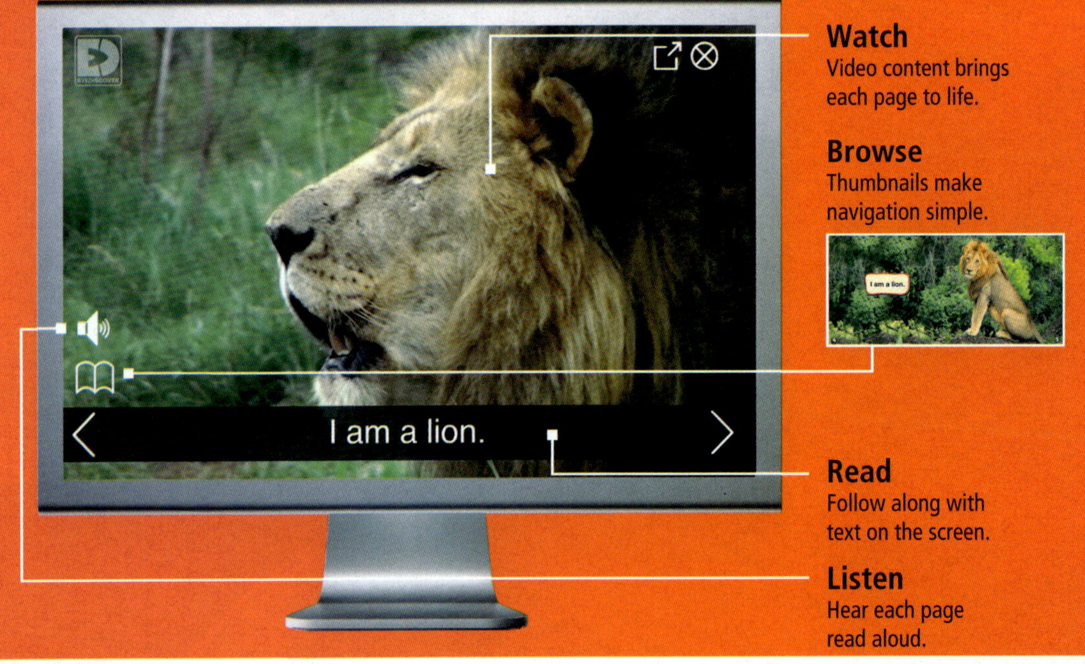

Watch
Video content brings each page to life.

Browse
Thumbnails make navigation simple.

Read
Follow along with text on the screen.

Listen
Hear each page read aloud.

Your EYEDISCOVER Optic Readalongs come alive with...

Audio
Listen to the entire book read aloud.

Video
High resolution videos turn each spread into an optic readalong.

OPTIMIZED FOR

- ✓ TABLETS
- ✓ WHITEBOARDS
- ✓ COMPUTERS
- ✓ AND MUCH MORE!

Planets

In this book, you will learn which planet

- is farthest from the Sun
- has the tallest mountain
- is known for its rings

and much more!

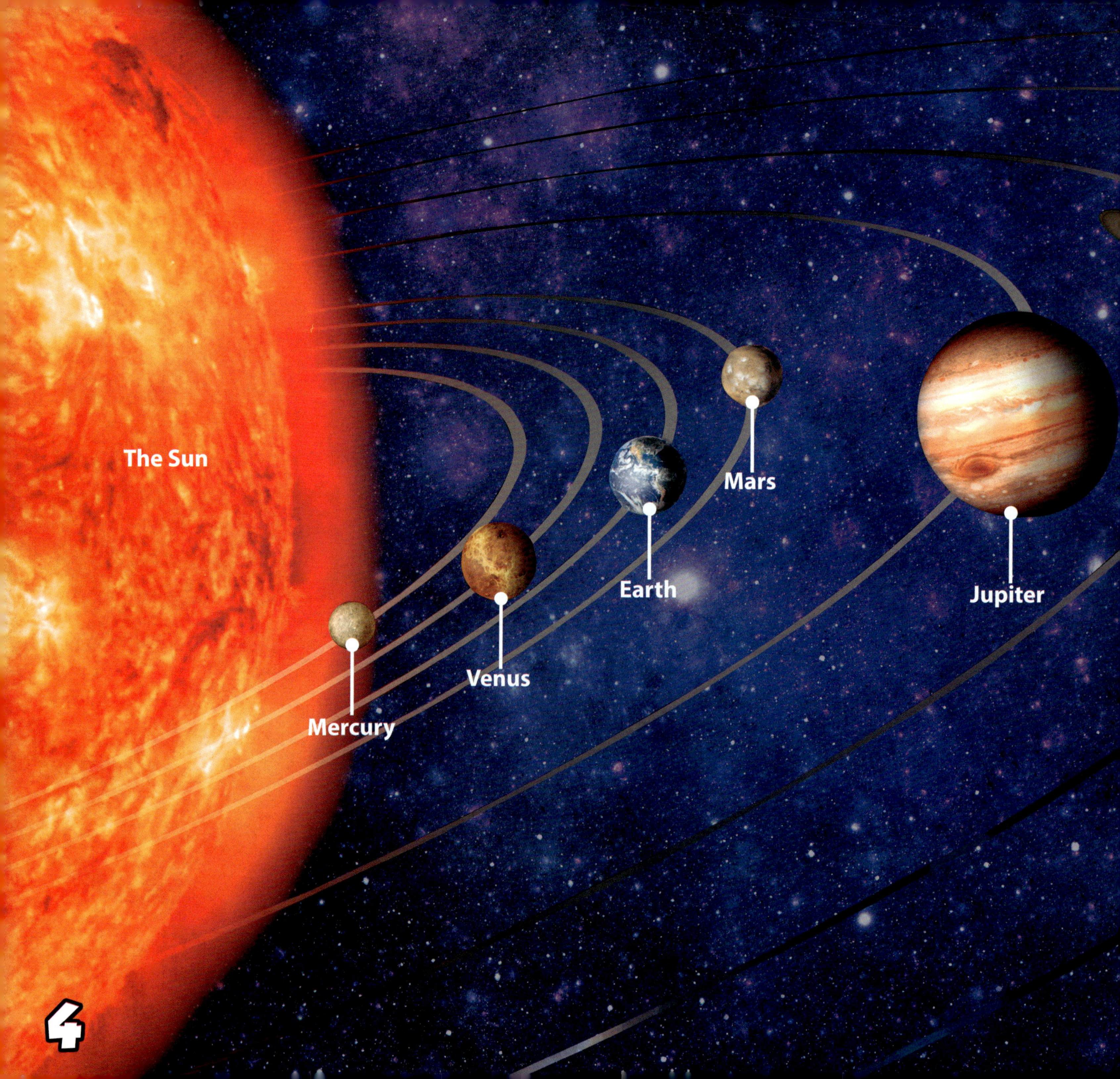
The Sun
Mercury
Venus
Earth
Mars
Jupiter

Eight planets circle the Sun. They are Mercury, Venus, Earth, Mars, Jupiter, Saturn, Uranus, and Neptune.

Mercury is closer to the Sun than any other planet. This makes it hard to see.

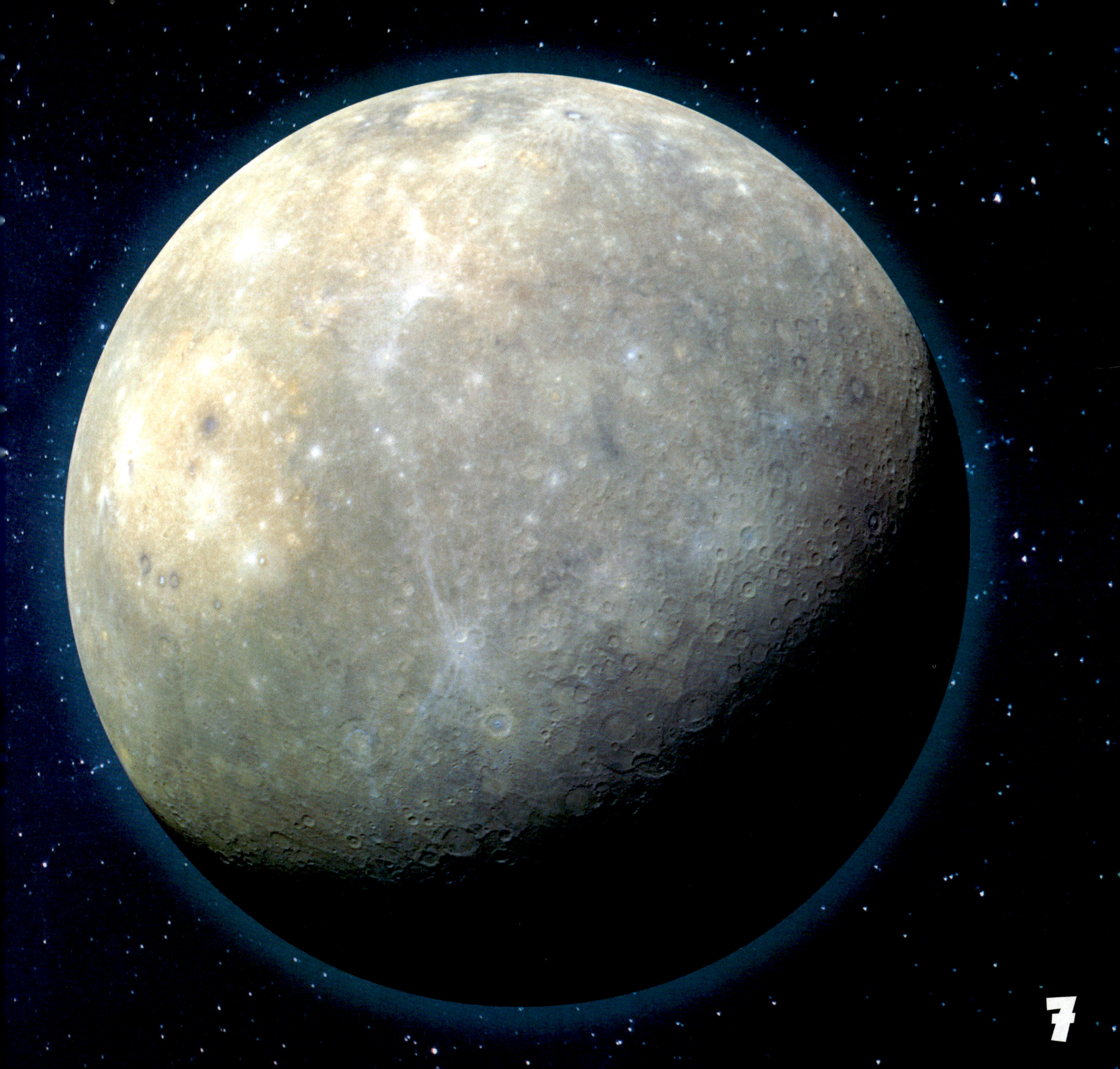

Venus is the hottest of all the planets. It is one of the brightest things in the night sky.

Earth is the only planet to have life. The main reason for this is that Earth has water.

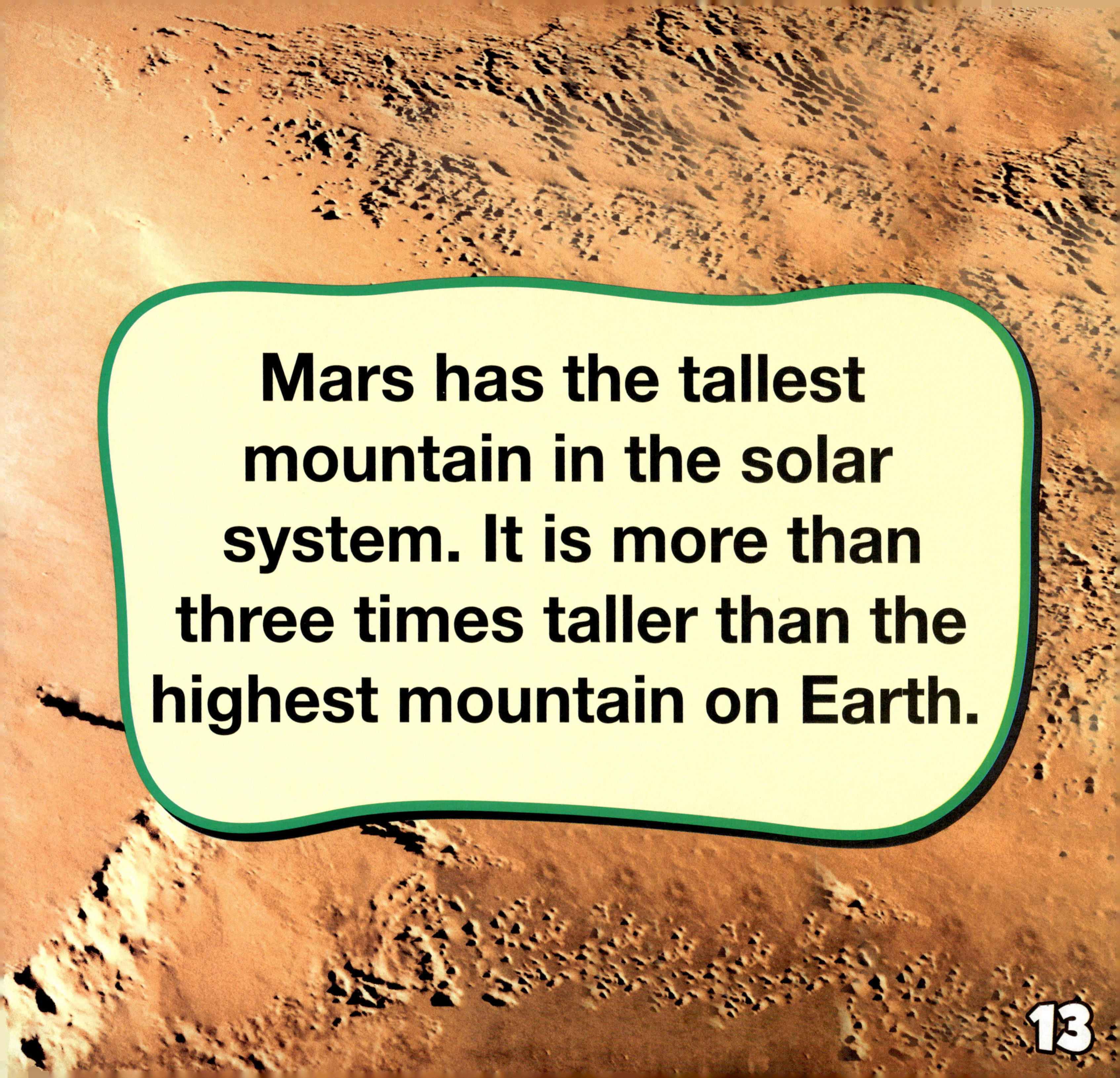

Mars has the tallest mountain in the solar system. It is more than three times taller than the highest mountain on Earth.

Jupiter is the largest planet. It is so big that all the other planets could fit inside it.

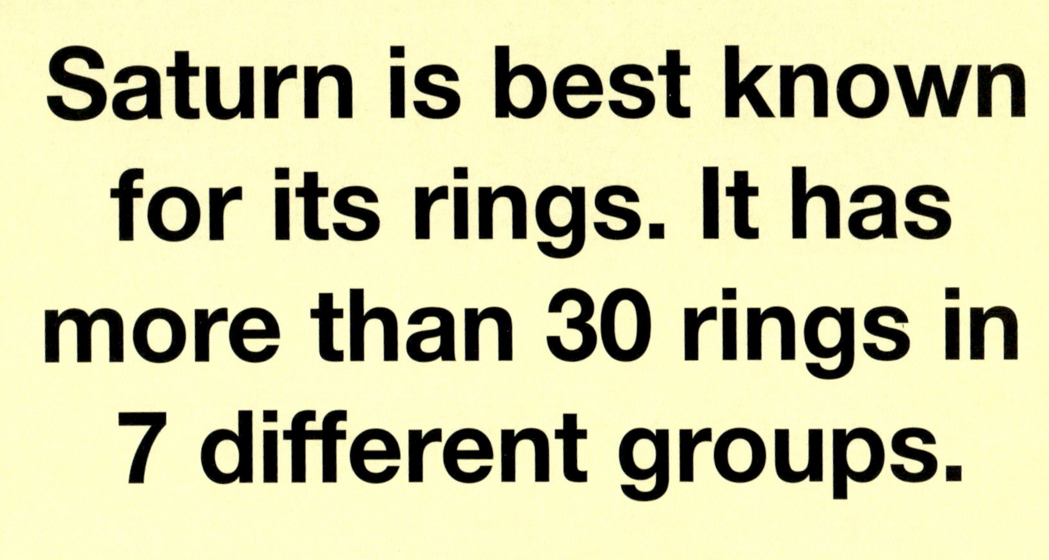

Saturn is best known for its rings. It has more than 30 rings in 7 different groups.

Uranus is the only planet that is tilted on its side. It moves very slowly.

Neptune is colder and farther from the Sun than any other planet.

Earth was made **4.54 billion years** ago.

A **year on Mercury** is only **88 Earth days** long.

Venus has **more than 1,600 volcanoes**. This is more than any other planet.

Saturn's rings are **wide** and very **thin.** They **stretch** more than **75,000 miles** (120,700 kilometers), but are only **66 feet** (20 meters) **thick.**

Uranus was thought to be a **comet** at first. It was found to be a planet in **1781.**

A person could leap **three times higher** on **Mars** than on **Earth.**

KEY WORDS

Research has shown that as much as 65 percent of all written material published in English is made up of 300 words. These 300 words cannot be taught using pictures or learned by sounding them out. They must be recognized by sight. This book contains 45 common sight words to help young readers improve their reading fluency and comprehension. This book also teaches young readers several important content words, such as proper nouns. These words are paired with pictures to aid in learning and improve understanding.

Page	Sight Words First Appearance
5	and, are, Earth, the, they
6	any, closer, hard, is, it, makes, other, see, than, this, to
9	all, in, night, of, one, things
10	for, has, have, life, only, that, water
13	more, mountain, on, three, times
14	big, could, so
17	different, groups, its, known
18	moves, side, very
21	from

Page	Content Words First Appearance
5	Jupiter, Mars, Mercury, Neptune, planets, Saturn, Sun, Uranus, Venus
9	sky
10	reason
13	solar system
17	rings

Watch
Video content brings each page to life.

Browse
Thumbnails make navigation simple.

Read
Follow along with text on the screen.

Listen
Hear each page read aloud.

Go to www.eyediscover.com and enter this book's unique code.

BOOK CODE

X274953